Poetry for Poetry's Sake

A. C. Bradley

ESPRIOS DIGITAL PUBLISHING

Poetry For Poetry's Sake

AN INAUGURAL LECTURE

DELIVERED ON JUNE 5, 1901

BY

A. C. BRADLEY, M.A., LL. D.

PROFESSOR OF POETRY IN THE UNIVERSITY OF
OXFORD FORMERLY FELLOW OF BALLIOL
COLLEGE

NOTE. —This Lecture is printed almost as it was delivered. I am aware that, especially in the earlier pages, difficult subjects are treated in a manner far too summary, but they require an exposition so full that it would destroy the original form of the Lecture, while a slight expansion would do little to provide against misunderstandings.

A. C. B.

POETRY FOR POETRY'S SAKE

One who, after twenty years, is restored to the University where he was taught and first tried to teach, and who has received at the hands of his Alma Mater an honour of which he never dreamed, is tempted to speak both of himself and of her. But I remember that you have come to listen to my thoughts about a great subject, and not to my feelings about myself; and, of Oxford, who that holds this Professorship could dare to speak, when he recalls the exquisite verse in which one of his predecessors described her beauty, and the prose in which he gently touched on her illusions and protested that they were as nothing when set against her age-long warfare with the Philistine? How, again, remembering him and others, should I venture to praise my predecessors? It would be pleasant to do so, and even pleasanter to me and you if, instead of lecturing, I quoted to you some of their best passages. But I could not do this for five years. Sooner or later, my own words would have to come, and the inevitable contrast. Not to sharpen it now, I will be silent concerning them also; and will only assure you that I do not forget them, or the greatness of the honour of succeeding them, or the responsibility which it entails.

Since I left Oxford one change has taken place in its educational system which may be thought to affect the Professorship of Poetry. A School of English Language and Literature has been founded, and has attracted a fair number of candidates. Naturally I rejoice in this change, knowing from experience the value of these studies; and

1

knowing also from experience, if I may speak boldly, how idle is that dream which flits about in Oxford and whispers that the mastering of Old English, on the basis of Teutonic phonology, and the conquest of the worlds opened by Chaucer and Shakespeare and Swift and Burke and twenty more, is a business too slight and a discipline not severe enough for undergraduates. I should be glad to lighten their labours, and, if it should seem advisable to those who can judge, I propose to give in one of the three Terms of the year, in addition to my statutory lecture, a few others intended specially for those who are reading for the School of English. I wish I could do more, but I resigned my chair in Glasgow with a view to work of another kind, and I could not have parted from my students there, to whom I am bound by ties of the most grateful affection, in order to take up similar duties even in the University of Oxford.

The charming poem with which my predecessor opened his literary career, and his admirable contributions to poetical history and criticism, prove that it would have been easy to him to devote his lectures to the interpretation of particular poets and poems. I believe, however, that he thought it better to confine himself chiefly to questions in Poetics or Aesthetics. I can well understand his choice; but, partly because he made it, I propose to make another, and to discuss these questions, if at all, only as they are illustrated by particular writers and works. Still in an inaugural lecture it is customary to take some wider subject; and so I fear you may have to-day to lament the truth of Addison's remark: 'There is nothing in nature so irksome as general discourses, especially when they turn chiefly upon words. ' Mine turns entirely upon words.

[Sidenote: POETRY]

The words 'Poetry for poetry's sake' recall the famous phrase 'Art for Art. ' It is far from my purpose to examine the possible meanings of that phrase, or all the questions it involves. I propose to state briefly what I understand by 'Poetry for poetry's sake, ' and then, after guarding against one or two misapprehensions of the formula, to consider more fully a single problem connected with it. And I must premise, without attempting to justify them, certain explanations. We are to consider poetry in its essence, and apart from the flaws which in most poems accompany their poetry. We are to include in the idea of poetry the metrical form, and not to regard this as a mere accident or a mere vehicle. And, finally, poetry being poems, we are to think of a poem as it actually exists; and, without aiming here at accuracy, we may say that an actual poem is the succession of experiences—sounds, images, thoughts, emotions—through which we pass when we are reading as poetically as we can. Of course this imaginative experience—if I may use the phrase for brevity—differs with every reader and every time of reading: a poem exists in innumerable degrees. But that insurmountable fact lies in the nature of things and does not concern us now.

What then does the formula 'Poetry for poetry's sake' tell us about this experience? It says, as I understand it, these things. First, this experience is an end in itself, is worth having on its own account, has an intrinsic value. Next, its *poetic* value is this intrinsic worth alone. Poetry may have also an ulterior value as a means to culture or religion; because it conveys instruction, or softens the passions, or furthers a good cause; because it brings the poet fame or money or a quiet conscience. So much the better: let it be valued for these reasons too. But its ulterior worth neither is nor can directly determine its poetic worth as a satisfying imaginative experience; and this is to be judged entirely from within. And to these two positions the formula would add, though not of necessity, a third. The consideration of ulterior ends, whether by the poet in the act of composing or by the reader in the act of experiencing, tends to lower poetic value. It does so because it tends to change the nature of poetry by taking it out of its own atmosphere. For its nature is to be not a part, nor yet a copy, of the real world (as we commonly understand that phrase), but to be a world by itself, independent, complete, autonomous; and to possess it fully you must enter that world, conform to its laws, and ignore for the time the beliefs, aims, and particular conditions which belong to you in the other world of reality.

[Sidenote: POETIC VALUE INTRINSIC]

Of the more serious misapprehensions to which these statements may give rise I will glance only at one or two. The offensive consequences often drawn from the formula 'Art for Art' will be found to attach not to the doctrine that Art is an end in itself, but to the doctrine that Art is the whole or supreme end of human life. And as this latter doctrine, which seems to me absurd, is in any case quite different from the former, its consequences fall outside my subject. The formula 'Poetry is an end in itself' has nothing to say on the many questions of moral judgement which arise from the fact that poetry has its place in a many-sided life. For anything it says, the intrinsic value of poetry might be so small, and its ulterior effects so mischievous, that it had better not exist. The formula only tells us that we must not place in antithesis poetry and human good, for poetry is one kind of human good; and that we must not determine the intrinsic value of this kind of good by direct reference to another. If we do, we shall find ourselves maintaining what we did not expect. If poetic value lies in the stimulation of religious feelings, *Lead, kindly Light* is no better a poem than many a tasteless version of a Psalm: if in the excitement of patriotism, why is *Scots, wha hae* superior to *We don't want to fight*? if in the mitigation of the passions, the Odes of Sappho will win but little praise: if in instruction, Armstrong's *Art of preserving Health* should win much.

Again, our formula may be accused of cutting poetry away from its connexion with life. And this accusation raises so huge a problem that I must ask leave to be dogmatic as well as brief. There is plenty of connexion between life and poetry, but it is, so to say, a connexion underground. The two may be called different forms of the same thing: one of them having (in the usual sense) reality, but seldom fully satisfying imagination; while the other offers something which satisfies imagination but has not (in the usual sense) full reality. They are parallel developments which nowhere meet, or, if I may use incorrectly a word which will be useful later, they are analogues. Hence we understand one by help of the other, and even, in a sense, care for one because of the other; but hence also, poetry neither is life, nor, strictly speaking, a copy of it. They differ not only because one has more mass and the other a more perfect shape; but they have different *kinds* of existence. The one touches us as beings occupying a given position in space and time, and having feelings, desires, and purposes due to that position: it appeals to imagination, but appeals to much besides. What meets us in poetry has not a position in the same series of time and space, or, if it has or had such a position, is taken apart from much that belonged to it there; and therefore it makes no direct appeal to those feelings, desires, and purposes, but speaks only to contemplative imagination—imagination the reverse of empty or emotionless, imagination saturated with the results of 'real' experience, but still contemplative. Thus, no doubt, one main reason why poetry has poetic value for us is that it presents to us in its own way something which we meet in another form in nature or life; and yet the test of its poetic value lies simply in the question whether it satisfies our imagination, the rest of us, our knowledge or conscience, for example, judging it only so far as they appear transmuted in our imagination. So also Shakespeare's knowledge or his moral insight, Milton's greatness of soul, Shelley's 'hate of hate' and 'love of love, ' and that desire to help men by his poetry which influenced this poet or that—not, surely, in the process of composition but in hours of meditation—all these have, as such, no poetical worth: they have that worth only when, passing through the unity of the poet's being, they reappear as qualities of imagination, and then are indeed mighty powers in the world of poetry.

I come to a third misapprehension, and so to my main subject. This formula, it is said, empties poetry of its meaning: it is really a doctrine of form for form's sake.

[Sidenote: WHERE DOES IT LIE?]

'It matters not what a poet says, so long as he says the thing well. The *what* is poetically indifferent: it is the *how* that counts. Matter, subject, content, substance, determines nothing; there is no subject with which poetry may not deal: the form, the treatment, is everything. Nay, more: not only is the matter indifferent, but it is the secret of Art to "eradicate the matter by means of the form. "' Phrases and statements like these meet us everywhere in current criticism of literature and the other arts. They are the stock-in-trade of writers who understand of them little more than the fact that somehow or other they are not 'bourgeois. ' But we find them also seriously used by writers whom we must respect, whether they are anonymous or not; something like one or another of them might be quoted, for example, from Professor Saintsbury, the late R. A. M. Stevenson, Schiller, Goethe himself; and they are the watchwords of a school in the one country where Aesthetics has flourished. They come, as a rule, from men who either practise one of the arts, or, from study of it, are interested in its methods. The general reader—a being so general that I may say what I will of him—is outraged by them. He feels that he is being robbed of almost all that he cares for in a work of art. 'You are asking me, ' he says, 'to look at the Dresden Madonna as if it were a Persian rug. You are telling me that the poetic value of *Hamlet* lies solely in its style and versification, and that my interest in the man and his fate is only an intellectual or moral interest. You pretend that, if I want to enjoy the poetry of *Crossing the Bar*, I must not mind what Tennyson says there, but must consider solely how he says it. But in that case I can care no more for a poem than I do for a set of nonsense verses; and I do not believe that the authors of *Hamlet* and *Crossing the Bar* regarded their poems thus. '

These antitheses of subject, matter, substance on the one side, form, treatment, handling on the other, are the field through which I especially want, in this lecture, to indicate a way. It is a field of battle; and the battle is waged for no trivial cause; but the cries of the combatants are terribly ambiguous. Those phrases of the so-called formalist may each mean five or six different things. If they mean one, they seem to me chiefly true; taken as the general reader not unnaturally takes them, they seem to me false and mischievous. It would be absurd to pretend that I can end in a few minutes a controversy which concerns the ultimate nature of Art, and leads perhaps to problems not yet soluble; but we can at least draw some plain distinctions which, in this controversy, are too often confused.

In the first place, then, let us take 'subject' in one particular sense; let us understand by it that which we have in view when, looking at the title of a poem, we say

8

that the poet has chosen this or that for his subject. The subject, in this sense, so far as I can discover, is generally something, real or imaginary, as it exists in the minds of fairly cultivated people. The subject of *Paradise Lost* would be the story of the Fall as that story exists in the general imagination of a Bible-reading people. The subject of Shelley's stanzas *To a Skylark* would be the ideas which arise in the mind of an educated person when, without knowing the poem, he hears the word 'skylark. ' If the title of a poem conveys little or nothing to us, the 'subject' appears to be either what we should gather by investigating the title in a dictionary or other book of the kind, or else such a brief suggestion as might be offered by a person who had read the poem, and who said, for example, that the subject of *The Ancient Mariner* was a sailor who killed an albatross and suffered for his deed.

[Sidenote: VALUE NOT IN SUBJECT]

Now the subject, in this sense (and I intend to use the word in no other), is not, as such, inside the poem, but outside it. The contents of the stanzas *To a Skylark* are not the ideas suggested by the word 'skylark' to the average man; they belong to Shelley just as much as the language does. The subject, therefore, is not the matter *of* the poem at all; and its opposite is not the *form* of the poem, but the whole poem. The subject is one thing; the poem, matter and form alike, another thing. This being so, it is surely obvious that the poetic value cannot lie in the subject, but lies entirely in its opposite, the poem. How can the subject determine the value when on one and the same subject poems may be written of all degrees of merit and demerit; or when a perfect poem may be composed on a subject so slight as a pet sparrow, and, if Macaulay may be trusted, a nearly worthless poem on a subject so stupendous as the omnipresence of the Deity? The 'formalist' is here perfectly right. Nor is he insisting on something unimportant. He is contending against our tendency to take the work of art as a mere copy or reminder of something already in our heads, or at the best as a suggestion of some idea as little removed as possible from the familiar. The sightseer who promenades a picture-gallery, remarking that this portrait is so like his cousin, or that landscape the very image of his birthplace, or who, after satisfying himself that one picture is about Elijah, passes on rejoicing to discover the subject, and nothing but the subject, of the next—what is he but an extreme example of this tendency? Well, but the very same tendency vitiates much of our criticism, much criticism of Shakespeare, for example, which, with all its cleverness and partial truth, still shows that the critic never passed from his own mind into Shakespeare's; and it may still be traced even in so fine a critic as Coleridge, as when he dwarfs the sublime struggle of Hamlet into the image of his own unhappy weakness. Hazlitt by no means escaped its influence. Only the third of that great trio, Lamb, appears almost always to have rendered the conception of the composer.

Again, it is surely true that we cannot determine beforehand what subjects are fit for Art, or name any subject on which a good poem might not possibly be written. To divide subjects into two groups, the beautiful or elevating, and the ugly or vicious, and to judge poems according as their subjects belong to one of these groups or the other, is to fall into the same pit, to confuse with our pre-conceptions the meaning of the poet. What the thing is in the poem he is to be judged by, not by the thing as it was before he touched it; and how can we venture to say beforehand that he cannot make a true poem out of something which to us was merely alluring or dull or revolting? The question whether, having done so, he ought to publish his poem; whether the thing in the poet's work will not be still confused by the incompetent Puritan or the incompetent sensualist with the thing in *his* mind, does not touch this point; it is a further question, one of ethics, not of art. No doubt the upholders of 'Art for art's sake' will generally be in favour of the courageous course, of refusing to sacrifice the better or stronger part of the public to the weaker or worse; but their maxim in no way binds them to this view. Dante Rossetti suppressed one of the best of his sonnets, a sonnet chosen for admiration by Tennyson, himself extremely sensitive about the moral effect of poetry; suppressed it, I believe, because it was called fleshly. One may regret Rossetti's judgement and at the same time admire his scrupulousness; but in any case he judged in his capacity of citizen, not in his capacity of artist.

[Sidenote: SUBJECT NOT INDIFFERENT]

So far then the 'formalist' appears to be right. But he goes too far, I think, if he maintains that the subject is indifferent and that all subjects are the same to poetry. And he does not prove his point by observing that a good poem might be written on a pin's head, and a bad one on the Fall of Man. That shows that the subject *settles* nothing, but not that it counts for nothing. The Fall of Man is really a more favourable subject than a pin's head. The Fall of Man, that is to say, offers opportunities of poetic effects wider in range and more penetrating in appeal. And the truth is that such a subject, as it exists in the general imagination, has some aesthetic value before the poet touches it. It is, as you may choose to call it, an inchoate poem or the débris of a poem. It is not an abstract idea or a bare isolated fact, but an assemblage of figures, scenes, actions, and events, which already appeal to emotional imagination; and it is already in some degree organized and formed. In spite of this a bad poet would make a bad poem on it; but then we should say he was unworthy of the subject. And we should not say this if he wrote a bad poem on a pin's head. Conversely, a good poem on a pin's head would almost certainly revolutionize its subject far more than a good poem on the Fall of Man. It might transform its subject so completely that we should say, 'The subject may be a pin's head, but the substance of the poem has very little to do with it.'

This brings us to another and different antithesis. Those figures, scenes, events, that form part of the subject called the Fall of Man, are not the substance of *Paradise Lost*; but in *Paradise Lost* there are figures, scenes, and events resembling them in some degree. These, with much more of the same kind, may be described as its substance, and may then be contrasted with the measured language of the poem, which will be called its form. Subject is the opposite not of form but of the whole poem. Substance is within the poem, and its opposite, form, is also within the poem. I am not criticizing this antithesis at present, but evidently it is quite different from the other. It is practically the distinction used in the old-fashioned criticism of epic and drama, and it flows down, not unsullied, from Aristotle. Addison, for example, in examining *Paradise Lost* considers in order the fable, the characters, and the sentiments; these will be the substance: then he considers the language, that is, the style and numbers; this will be the form. In like manner, the substance or meaning of a lyric may be distinguished from the form.

[Sidenote: SUBSTANCE AND FORM]

Now I believe it will be found that a large part of the controversy we are dealing with arises from a confusion between these two distinctions of substance and form, and of subject and poem. The extreme formalist lays his whole weight on the form because he thinks its opposite is the mere subject. The general reader is angry, but makes the same mistake, and gives to the subject praises that rightly belong to the substance[1]. I will read an example of what I mean. I can only explain the following words of a good critic by supposing that for the moment he has fallen into this confusion: 'The mere matter of all poetry—to wit, the appearances of nature and the thoughts and feelings of men—being unalterable, it follows that the difference between poet and poet will

13

depend upon the manner of each in applying language, metre, rhyme, cadence, and what not, to this invariable material. ' What has become here of the substance of *Paradise Lost*—the story, scenery, characters, sentiments as they are in the poem? They have vanished clean away. Nothing is left but the form on one side, and on the other not even the subject, but a supposed invariable material, the appearances of nature and the thoughts and feelings of men. Is it surprising that the whole value should then be found in the form?

So far we have assumed that this antithesis of substance and form is valid, and that it always has one meaning. In reality it has several, but we will leave it in its present shape, and pass to the question of its validity. And this question we are compelled to raise, because we have to deal with the two contentions that the poetic value lies wholly or mainly in the substance, and that it lies wholly or mainly in the form. Now these contentions, whether false or true, may seem at least to be clear; but we shall find, I think, that they are both of them false, or both of them nonsense: false if they concern anything outside the poem, nonsense if they apply to something in it. For what do they evidently imply? They imply that there are in a poem two parts, factors, or components, a substance and a form; and that you can conceive them distinctly and separately, so that when you are speaking of the one you are not speaking of the other. Otherwise how can you ask the question, In which of them does the value lie? But really in a poem, apart from defects, there are no such factors or components; and therefore it is strictly nonsense to ask in which of them the value lies. And on the other hand, if the substance and the form referred to are not in the poem, then both the contentions are false, for its poetic value lies in itself.

[Sidenote: IDENTITY OF SUBSTANCE AND FORM]

What I mean is neither new nor mysterious; and it will be clear, I believe, to any one who reads poetry poetically and who closely examines his experience. When you are reading a poem, I would ask—not analysing it, and much less criticizing it, but allowing it, as it proceeds, to make its full impression on you through the exertion of your re-creating imagination—do you then apprehend and enjoy as one thing a certain meaning or substance, and as another thing certain articulate sounds, and do you somehow compound these two? Surely you do not, any more than you apprehend apart, when you see some one smile, those lines in the face which express a feeling, and the feeling that the lines express. Just as there the lines and their meaning are to you one thing, not two, so in poetry the meaning and the sounds are one: there is, if I may put it so, a resonant meaning, or a meaning resonance. If you read the line, 'The sun is warm, the sky is clear, ' you do not experience separately the image of a warm sun and clear sky, on the one side, and certain unintelligible rhythmical sounds on the other; nor yet do you experience them together, side by side; but you experience the one *in* the other. And in like manner when you are really reading *Hamlet*, the action and the characters are not something which you conceive apart from the words; you apprehend them from point to point *in* the words. Afterwards, no doubt, when you are out of the poetic experience, but remember it, you may by analysis decompose this unity, and attend to a substance more or less isolated, and a form more or less isolated. But these are things in your analytic head, not in the poem, which is *poetic* experience. And if you want to have the poem again, you cannot find it by adding together these two products of decomposition; you can only find it by passing back into poetic experience. And then what you have again is no aggregate of factors, it is a unity in which you can no more separate a substance and a form than you can separate living blood and the life in the blood. This unity has, if you like, various 'aspects' or 'sides, ' but they are not factors or parts; if you try to examine one, you find it is also the other. Call them substance and form if you please, but these are not the reciprocally exclusive substance and form to which the two contentions *must* refer. They do not 'agree, ' for they are not apart: they are one thing from different points of view, and in that sense identical. And this identity of content and form, you will say, is no accident; it is of the essence of poetry in so far as it is poetry, and of all art in so far as it is art. Just as there is in music not sound on one side and a meaning on the other, but expressive sound, and if you ask what is the meaning you can only answer by pointing to the sounds; just as in painting there is not a meaning *plus* paint, but a meaning *in* paint, or significant paint, and no man can really express the meaning in any other way than in paint and in *this* paint; so in a poem the true content and the true form neither exist nor can be imagined apart. When then you are asked whether the value of a poem lies in a substance got by decomposing the poem and present, as such, only in reflective analysis, or in a form arrived at and existing in the same way, you will answer, 'It lies neither in one, nor in the other, nor in any addition of them, but in the poem, where they are not. ' And when you are told that you are talking *a priori* metaphysics, you will not mind. 'Metaphysics' does not mean anything. It is only a term of abuse applied to the effort to look at facts instead of repeating *a priori* fictions.

We have then, first, an antithesis of subject and poem. This is clear and valid; and the question in which of them does the value lie is intelligible; and its answer is, In the poem. We have next a distinction of substance and form. If the substance means ideas, images, and the like taken alone, and the form means the measured language taken by itself, this is a possible distinction, but it is a distinction of things not in the poem, and the value lies in neither of them. If substance and form mean anything *in* the poem, then each is involved in the other, and the question in which of them the value lies has no sense. No doubt you may say, speaking loosely and perilously, that in this poet or poem the aspect of substance is the more noticeable, and in that the aspect of form, and you may pursue interesting discussions on this basis: but no principle or ultimate question of value is touched by them. And apart from that question, of course, I am not denying the usefulness and necessity of the distinction. We cannot dispense with it. To consider separately the action or the characters of a play, and separately its style or versification, is both legitimate and valuable, so long as we remember what we are doing. But the true critic in speaking of these apart never really thinks of them apart;

the whole, the poetic experience, of which they are but aspects, is always in his mind; and he is always aiming at a richer, truer, more intense repetition of that experience. On the other hand, when the question of principle, of poetic value, is raised, these aspects *must* fall apart into components, separately conceivable; and then there arise two heresies, equally false, that the value lies in one of two things, both of which are outside the poem where its value cannot lie.

[Sidenote: SUBSTANCE]

On the heresy of the separable substance a few additional words will suffice. This heresy is seldom formulated, but perhaps some unconscious holder of it may object: 'Surely the action and the characters of *Hamlet* are in the play; and surely I can retain these, though I have forgotten all the words. I admit that I do not possess the whole poem, but I possess a part, and the most important part. ' And I would answer: 'If we are not concerned with any question of principle, I accept all that you say except the last words, which do raise such a question. Speaking loosely, I agree that the action and characters, as you perhaps conceive them, together with a great deal more, are in the poem. Even then, however, you must not claim to possess all of this kind that is in the poem; for in forgetting the words you must have lost innumerable details of the action and the characters. And, when the question of value is raised, I must insist that the action and characters, as you conceive them, are not in *Hamlet* at all. If they are, point them out. You cannot do it. What you find at any moment of that succession of experiences

18

called *Hamlet* is words. In these words, to speak loosely again, the action and characters (more of them than you can conceive apart) are focussed; but your experience is not a combination of them, as ideas, on the one side, with certain sounds on the other; it is an experience of something in which the two are indissolubly fused. If you deny this, to be sure I can make no answer, or can only answer that I have reason to believe that you cannot read poetically, or else are misinterpreting your experience. But if you do not deny this, then you will admit that the action and characters of the poem, as you separately imagine them, are no part of it, but a product of it in your reflective imagination, a faint analogue of one aspect of it taken in detachment from the whole. Well, I do not deny, I would even insist, that, in the case of so long a poem as *Hamlet*, it may be necessary from time to time to interrupt the poetic experience, in order to enrich it by forming such a product and dwelling on it. Nor, in a wide sense of "poetic, " do I question the poetic value of this product, as you think of it apart from the poem. It resembles our recollections of the heroes of history or legend, who move about in our imaginations, "forms more real than living man, " and are worth much to us though we do not remember anything they said. Our ideas and images of the "substance" of a poem have this poetic value, and more, if they are at all adequate. But they cannot determine the poetic value of the poem, for (not to speak of the competing claims of the "form") nothing that is outside the poem can do that, and they, as such, are outside it[2]. '

[Sidenote: STYLE]

Let us turn to the so-called form—style and versification. There is no such thing as mere form in poetry. All form is expression. Style may have indeed a certain aesthetic worth in partial abstraction from the particular matter it conveys, as in a well-built sentence you may take pleasure in the build almost apart from the meaning. Even then style is expressive—presents to sense, for example, the order, ease, and rapidity with which ideas move in the writer's mind—but it is not expressive of the meaning of that particular sentence. And it is possible, interrupting poetic experience, to decompose it and abstract for comparatively separate consideration this nearly formal element of style. But the aesthetic value of style so taken is not considerable; you could not read with pleasure for an hour a composition which had no other merit. And in poetic experience you never apprehend this value by itself; the style is here expressive also of a particular meaning, or rather is one aspect of that unity whose other aspect is meaning. So that what you apprehend may be called indifferently an expressed meaning or a significant form. Perhaps on this point I may in Oxford appeal to authority, that of Matthew Arnold and Walter Pater, the latter at any rate an authority whom the formalist will not despise. What is the gist of Pater's teaching about style, if it is not that in the end the one virtue of style is truth or adequacy; that the word, phrase, sentence, should express perfectly the writer's perception, feeling, image, or thought; so that, as we read a descriptive phrase of Keats's, we exclaim, 'That is the thing itself'; so that, to quote Arnold, the words are 'symbols equivalent with the thing symbolized, ' or, in our technical language, a form identical with its content?

Hence in true poetry it is, in strictness, impossible to express the meaning in any but its own words, or to change the words without changing the meaning. A translation of such poetry is not really the old meaning in a fresh dress; it is a new product, something like the poem, though, if one chooses to say so, more like it in the aspect of meaning than in the aspect of form.

No one who understands poetry, it seems to me, would dispute this, were it not that, falling away from his experience, or misled by theory, he takes the word 'meaning' in a sense almost ludicrously inapplicable to poetry. People say, for instance, 'steed' and 'horse' have the same meaning; and in bad poetry they have, but not in poetry that *is* poetry.

'Bring forth the horse! ' The horse was brought:
In truth he was a noble steed!

says Byron in *Mazeppa*. If the two words mean the same here, transpose them:

'Bring forth the steed! ' The steed was brought:
In truth he was a noble horse!

and ask again if they mean the same. Or let me take a line certainly very free from 'poetic diction':

To be or not to be, that is the question.

You may say that this means the same as 'What is just now occupying my attention is the comparative disadvantages of continuing to live or putting an end to myself. ' And for practical purposes—the purpose, for example, of a coroner—it does. But as the second version altogether misrepresents the speaker at that moment of his existence, while the first does represent him, how can they for any but a practical or logical purpose be said to have the same sense? Hamlet was well able to 'unpack his heart with words, ' but he will not unpack it with our paraphrases.

[Sidenote: VERSIFICATION]

These considerations apply equally to versification. If I take the famous line which describes how the souls of the dead stood waiting by the river, imploring a passage from Charon:

Tendebantque manus ripae ulterioris amore,

and if I translate it, 'and were stretching forth their hands in longing for the further bank, ' the charm of the original has fled. Why has it fled? Partly (but we have dealt with that) because I have substituted for five words, and those the words of Virgil, twelve words, and those my own. In some measure because I have turned into rhythmless prose a line of verse which, as mere sound, has unusual beauty. But much more because in doing so I have also changed the *meaning* of Virgil's line. What that meaning is *I* cannot say: Virgil has said it. But I can see this much, that the translation conveys a far less vivid picture of the outstretched hands and of their remaining outstretched, and a far less poignant sense of the distance of the shore and the longing of the souls. And it does so partly because this picture and this sense are conveyed not only by the obvious meaning of the words, but through the long-drawn sound of 'Tendebantque, ' through the time occupied by the five syllables and therefore by the idea of 'ulterioris, ' and through the identity of the long sound 'or' in the penultimate syllables of 'ulterioris amore' — all this, and much more, apprehended not in this analytical fashion, nor as *added* to the beauty of mere sound and to the obvious meaning, but in unity with them and so as expressive of the poetic meaning of the whole.

It is always so in fine poetry. The value of versification, when it is indissolubly fused with meaning, can hardly be exaggerated. The gift for feeling it, even more perhaps than the gift for feeling the value of diction, is the *specific* gift for poetry, as distinguished from other arts. But versification, taken, as far as possible, all by itself, has a very different worth. Some aesthetic worth it has; how much, you may experience by reading poetry in a language of which you do not understand a syllable. The pleasure is quite appreciable, but it is not great; nor in actual poetic experience do you meet with it, as such, at all. For it is not *added* to the pleasure of the meaning when you read poetry that you do understand: by some mystery the music is then the music *of* the meaning, and the two are one. However fond of versification you might be, you would tire very soon of reading verses in Chinese; and before long of reading Virgil and Dante if you were ignorant of their languages. But take the music as it is *in* the poem, and there is a marvellous change. Now

It gives a very echo to the seat
Where Love is throned;

or 'carries far into your heart, ' almost like music itself,
the sound

Of old, unhappy, far-off things
And battles long ago.

What then is to be said of the following sentence of the
critic quoted before: 'But when any one who knows what
poetry is reads—

Our noisy years seem moments in the being
Of the eternal silence,

he sees that, quite independently of the meaning,... there
is one note added to the articulate music of the world—a
note that never will leave off resounding till the eternal
silence itself gulfs it'? I must think that the writer is
deceiving himself. For I could quite understand his
enthusiasm, if it were an enthusiasm for the music of the
meaning; but as for the music, 'quite independently of
the meaning, ' so far as I can hear it thus (and I doubt if
any one who knows English can quite do so), I find it
gives some pleasure, but only a trifling pleasure. And
indeed I venture to doubt whether, considered as mere
sound, the words are at all exceptionally beautiful, as
Virgil's line certainly is. Whatever may be the
consequence, I would back against them, 'quite
independently of the meaning, ' this once famous stanza:

Where is Cupid's crimson motion,
Billowy ecstasy of woe?
Bear me straight, meandering ocean,
Where the stagnant torrents flow.

[Sidenote: IMPERFECT UNITY]

When poetry answers to its idea and is purely or almost purely poetic, we find the identity of form and content; and the degree of purity attained may be tested by the degree in which we feel it hopeless to convey the effect of a poem or passage in any form but its own. Where the notion of doing so is simply ludicrous, you have quintessential poetry. But a great part even of good poetry, especially in long works, is of a mixed nature; and so we find in it no more than a partial agreement of a form and substance which remain to some extent distinct. This is so in many passages of Shakespeare (the greatest of poets when he chose, but not always a conscientious poet); passages where something was wanted for the sake of the plot, but he did not care about it or was hurried. The conception of the passage is then distinct from the execution, and neither is inspired. This is so also, I think, wherever we can truly speak of merely decorative effect. We seem to perceive that the poet had a truth or fact—philosophical, agricultural, social—distinctly before him, and then, as we say, clothed it in metrical and coloured language. Most argumentative, didactic, or satiric poems are partly of this kind; and in imaginative poems anything which is really a mere 'conceit' is mere decoration. We often deceive ourselves in this matter, for what we call decoration has often a new and genuinely poetic content of its own; but wherever there is mere decoration, we judge the poetry to be not wholly poetic. And so when Wordsworth inveighed against poetic diction, though he hurled his darts rather wildly, what he was rightly aiming at was a phraseology, not the living body of a new content, but the mere worn-out body of an old one.

In pure poetry it is otherwise. Pure poetry is not the decoration of a preconceived and clearly defined matter: it springs from the creative impulse of a vague imaginative mass pressing for development and definition. If the poet already knew exactly what he meant to say, why should he write the poem? The poem would in fact already be written. For only its completion can reveal, even to him, exactly what he wanted. When he began and while he was at work, he did not possess his meaning; it possessed him. It was not a fully formed soul asking for a body: it was an inchoate soul in the inchoate body of perhaps two or three vague ideas and a few scattered phrases. The growing of this body into its full stature and perfect shape was the same thing as the gradual self-definition of the meaning. And this is the reason why such poems strike us as creations, not manufactures, and have the magical effect which mere decoration cannot produce. This is also the reason why, if we insist on asking for the meaning of such a poem, we can only be answered 'It means itself. '

[Sidenote: THE TWO HERESIES]

26

And so at last I may explain why I have troubled myself and you with what may seem an arid controversy about mere words. It is not so. These heresies which would make poetry a compound of two factors—a matter common to it with the merest prose, *plus* a poetic form, as the one heresy says: a poetical substance *plus* a negligible form, as the other says—are not only untrue, they are injurious to the dignity of poetry. In an age already inclined to shrink from those higher realms where poetry touches religion and philosophy, the formalist heresy encourages men to taste poetry as they would a fine wine, which has indeed an aesthetic value, but a small one. And then the natural man, finding an empty form, hurls into it the matter of cheap pathos, rancid sentiment, vulgar humour, bare lust, ravenous vanity—everything which, in Schiller's phrase[3], the form should extirpate, but which no mere form can extirpate. And the other heresy—which is indeed rather a practise than a creed—encourages us in the habit so dear to us of putting our own thoughts or fancies into the place of the poet's creation. What he meant by *Hamlet*, or the *Ode to a Nightingale*, or *Abt Vogler*, we say, is this or that which we knew already; and so we lose what he had to tell us. But he meant what he said, and said what he meant.

Poetry in this matter is not, as good critics of painting and music often affirm, different from the other arts; in all of them the content is one thing with the form. What Beethoven meant by his symphony, or Turner by his picture, was not something which you can name, but the picture and the symphony. Meaning they have, but *what* meaning can be uttered in no language but their own:

and we know this, though some strange delusion makes us think the meaning has less worth, because we cannot put it into words. Well, it is just the same with poetry. But because poetry is words, we vainly fancy that some other words than its own will express its meaning. And they will do so no more—or, if you like to speak loosely, only a little more—than words will express the meaning of the Dresden Madonna. Something a little like it they may indeed express. And we may find analogues of the meaning of poetry outside it, which may help us to appropriate it. The other arts, the best ideas of philosophy or religion, much that nature and life offer us or force upon us, are akin to it. But they are only akin. Nor is it the expression of them. Poetry does not present to imagination our highest knowledge or belief, and much less our dreams and opinions; but it, content and form in unity, embodies in own irreplaceable way something which embodies itself also in other irreplaceable ways, such as philosophy or religion. And just as each of these gives a satisfaction which the other cannot possibly give, so we find in poetry, which cannot satisfy the needs they meet, that which by their natures they cannot afford us. But we shall not find it fully if we look for something else.

[Sidenote: THE FURTHER MEANING OF POETRY]

And yet, when all is said, the question will still recur, though now in quite another sense, What does poetry mean? This unique expression, which cannot be replaced by any other, still seems to be trying to express something beyond itself. And this, we feel, is also what the other arts, and religion, and philosophy are trying to express: and that is what impels us to seek in vain to translate the one into the other. About the best poetry, and not only the best, there floats an atmosphere of infinite suggestion. The poet speaks to us of one thing, but in this one thing there seems to lurk the secret of all. He said what he meant, but his meaning seems to beckon away beyond itself, or rather to expand into something boundless which is only focussed in it; something also which, we feel, would satisfy not only the imagination, but the whole of us; that something within us, and without, which everywhere

Makes us seem
To patch up fragments of a dream,
Part of which comes true, and part
Beats and trembles in the heart.

Those who are susceptible to this effect of poetry find it not only, perhaps not most, in the ideals which she has sometimes described, but in a child's song by Christina Rossetti about a mere crown of wind-flowers, and in tragedies like *Lear*, where the sun seems to have set for ever. They hear this spirit murmuring its undertone through the *Aeneid*, and catch its voice in the song of Keats's nightingale, and its light upon the figures on the Urn, and it pierces them no less in Shelley's hopeless lament, *O world, O life, O time*, than in the rapturous ecstasy of his *Life of Life*. This all-embracing perfection cannot be expressed in poetic words or words of any kind, nor yet in music or in colour, but the suggestion of it is in much poetry, if not all, and poetry has in this suggestion, this 'meaning, ' a great part of its value. We do it wrong, and we defeat our own purposes when we try to bend it to them:

We do it wrong, being so majestical,
To offer it the show of violence;
For it is as the air invulnerable,
And our vain blows malicious mockery.

It is a spirit. It comes we know not whence. It will not speak at our bidding, nor answer in our language. It is not our servant; it is our master.

FOOTNOTES.

[1] What is here called 'substance' is what people generally mean when they use the word 'subject. ' I am not arguing against this usage, or in favour of the usage which I have adopted for the sake of clearness. It does not matter which we employ, so long as we and others know what we mean.

[2] These remarks will hold good, *mutatis mutandis*, if by 'substance' is understood the 'moral' or the 'idea' of a poem, although perhaps in one instance out of five thousand this maybe found in so many words in the poem.

[3] Not that to Schiller 'form' meant mere style and versification.